DOGS WITH JOBS

Water Rescue Dogs

Helen Lepp Friesen

MEDIA ENHANCED BOOKS
AV2 BY WEIGL
ADDED VALUE • AUDIO VISUAL

www.av2books.com

Published by AV² by Weigl
350 5th Avenue, 59th Floor
New York, NY 10118
Website: www.av2books.com

Library of Congress Cataloging-in-Publication Data
Names: Friesen, Helen Lepp, 1961- author.
Title: Water rescue dogs / Helen Lepp Friesen.
Description: New York, NY : AV2 by Weigl, [2020] | Series: Dogs with jobs | Audience: Grade 4 to 6. | Includes index.
Identifiers: LCCN 2018053545 (print) | LCCN 2018054185 (ebook) | ISBN 9781489699534 (Multi User Ebook) | ISBN 9781489699541 (Single User Ebook) | ISBN 9781489699510 (hardcover : alk. paper) | ISBN 9781489699527 (softcover : alk. paper)
Subjects: LCSH: Water rescue dogs--Juvenile literature.
Classification: LCC SF428.55 (ebook) | LCC SF428.55 .F75 2020 (print) | DDC 636.7/0886--dc23
LC record available at https://lccn.loc.gov/2018053545

Printed in Guangzhou, China
1 2 3 4 5 6 7 8 9 0 23 22 21 20 19

012019
103118

Editor: Katie Gillespie   Art Director: Terry Paulhus

Weigl acknowledges Getty Images, Alamy, iStock, Shutterstock, and Wikimedia Commons as its primary image suppliers for this title.

CONTENTS

Four-Legged Heroes

Dogs can learn many new tricks. With training, some dogs learn how to be water rescue dogs. These dogs save people from drowning.

The most common water rescue dog **breed** is the Newfoundland. These giant dogs are good swimmers. They are very friendly and like being around humans.

Newfoundlands are sometimes called "Newfies" for short.

🐾 Other water-loving breeds are Portuguese water dogs and Labradors. They also make good water rescue dogs.

A Long History of Helping Out

In the past, Newfoundlands rode along on sailing ships. They were known as "ship dogs," who helped fishermen pull nets out of the ocean. Newfoundlands also pulled carts with heavy loads. They were obedient and hardworking animals.

More recently, Newfoundlands are best known for saving lives. Whizz was a famous **marine** rescue dog. He patrolled the Bristol Channel with the Royal Navy Rescue. Whizz saved hundreds of lives, and in 2007, he even rescued another dog from drowning. In 2016, this hero Newfoundland was given the **PDSA Order of Merit** in recognition of all his saves. He was the first to be **posthumously** presented with the honor.

Dogs at Work

A water rescue dog and his handler work as a team. If they are part of a Search and Rescue (SAR) Team, they may respond to calls. These calls can be to rescue a **victim** drowning in a lake or near a turned-over boat. The handler and her dog may have to take a boat or helicopter to the site.

SAR is a dangerous job. People respect water rescue dogs and their handlers for their bravery. The handler typically rewards the dog for his work.

Newfoundlands are sensitive dogs. They know when to be careful with **fragile** patients. Lifeguards can only rescue one or two drowning people at a time. Newfoundlands are very strong. They can pull up to 10 people out of the water all at once.

FACTS UNLEASHED

At a large scene, there may be **distractions** such as distraught family members or media. It is important for the dog not to get distracted in these stressful situations.

Water Rescue Dogs on Duty

Handlers and their dogs must pass a national certification to be able to work in SAR. They need to recertify regularly to keep their skills up to date. On duty, they respond to crisis situations. SAR missions can be in small lakes or large bodies of water. Dogs and handlers are both trained to work in many kinds of conditions and weather.

When a call comes in from the police, the handler prepares the tools needed for the rescue. These may include life rings, severe weather clothing, and blankets. When they arrive on the scene, a handler and her dog work as a team to rescue the victims.

Training

Before dogs can work as water rescue dogs, they need to be trained. This training can take up to two years. Once a dog is trained, there are a variety of jobs he can do.

The Newfoundland Club of America (NCA) developed the first water test for water rescue dogs. Most of the first trial test, held in June 1972, is still used today. A group of dedicated committee members developed the test. There are three levels. Dogs who accomplish the Junior Exercises receive the title of Water Dog (WD). Dogs who complete the Senior Exercises receive the title of Water Rescue Dog (WRD). Elite dogs can become Water Rescue Dog Excellent (WRDX).

The Senior Exercises require dogs to remember more than one command. In order of command, they have to fetch a life jacket and boat cushion. They also have to be able to jump into the water and fetch a paddle. If there are three swimmers in the water, the dog has to decide which one is drowning and carry a life ring to the correct person.

Dogs must listen to their handlers' commands about when to return to shore. They also have to find and fetch a bulky item from the water, and return it to their handlers. Other exercises include swimming out and delivering a rope to a drowning person, and going to an afloat boat and pulling it to shore.

FACTS UNLEASHED

Puppies start training to be water rescue dogs at about four months old. Handlers train their dog in phases, and play games such as hide and seek with them. The whole training period can take anywhere from six months to two years.

Heroic Gander

Many dogs have become well known for their heroic rescues. Water rescue dogs were sent along with soldiers in military operations. They traveled with the soldiers and were trained to sense danger. It was their job to protect the soldiers.

Gander was a heroic water rescue dog. He was stationed with the Royal Rifles of Canada. In 1941, during World War II, Gander traveled with his battalion to Hong Kong Island. He protected the soldiers, but his final brave act cost him his life.

In the Battle of Lye Mun, Gander noticed that a **grenade** had been tossed. It landed near a group of his soldiers. Gander ran and picked up the grenade to spare the soldiers' lives. The grenade exploded and Gander was killed instantly.

On October 27, 2000, long after his death, Gander was awarded the Dickin Medal, which was founded by Maria Dickin in 1943. The award honors extraordinarily brave animals serving with British Commonwealth forces. Gander's heroic act of bravery will be remembered for years to come.

Safety First

It is natural to want to pet a dog. However, if you see a water rescue dog, it is always best to ask first before you pet him. Newfoundland dogs are typically gentle and calm. If the owner agrees, it is fine to pet them. Water rescue dogs have an important job. You can even ask the owner about the dog's job and the kinds of tasks he performs.

FACTS UNLEASHED

The average height of a grown Newfoundland is between 26 and 28 inches (66 and 71 centimeters). These giant dogs can weigh up to 150 pounds (68 kilograms).

What Makes a Good Water Rescue Dog?

Water rescue dogs have certain traits that make them well suited for their jobs. They are good swimmers and are strong enough to pull a person out of the water. Newfoundlands have **webbed** toes, just like ducks. Instead of doing the usual doggie paddle like other dogs, they are able to move more quickly through the water because of their flipper-like paws. Although their fur is long, it is **waterproof**. Newfoundlands have fur that is like a thick coat. In cold water, it keeps them warm. Their healthy lung size helps them hold their breath to stay under water for a long time.

Quiz

1 Which dog breed is most commonly used for water rescues?

2 Which water rescue dog saved the lives of soldiers in World War II?

3 Which dog was given the PDSA Order of Merit in 2016?

4 What is a water rescue dog's trainer called?

5 What skills do good water rescue dogs have?

6 What are some things that water rescue dogs are trained to do?

7 How heavy can Newfoundlands get?

8 At what age do water rescue dogs start training?

9 What award did Gander receive?

10 What do water rescue dogs get when they complete a rescue?

ANSWERS

1 Newfoundland **2** Gander **3** Whizz **4** A handler **5** Being good swimmers and holding their breath for a long time **6** Fetch a life jacket and pull a person with a life ring **7** Up to 150 pounds (68 kg) **8** About four months old **9** Dickin Medal **10** A reward

Key Words

breed: a group of animals with similar characteristics that are descended from common ancestors

distractions: things that prevent full attention

fragile: easily broken

grenade: a small hand-held bomb

handler: a person who trains dogs

marine: trained to serve at sea

PDSA Order of Merit: an award given to service animals such as dogs and horses that recognizes their outstanding devotion and contributions to society

posthumously: after death

victim: a person in danger of harm

waterproof: safe from water damage

webbed: connected

Index

Log on to www.av2books.com

AV² by Weigl brings you media enhanced books that support active learning. Go to www.av2books.com, and enter the special code found on page 2 of this book. You will gain access to enriched and enhanced content that supplements and complements this book. Content includes video, audio, weblinks, quizzes, a slide show, and activities.

AV² Online Navigation

Audio
Listen to sections of the book read aloud.

Book Pages
AV² pages directly correspond to pages in the book.

Video
Watch informative video clips.

Embedded Weblinks
Gain additional information for research.

Key Words
Study vocabulary, and complete a matching word activity.

Try This!
Complete activities and hands-on experiments.

Quizzes
Test your knowledge.

Slide Show
View images and captions, and prepare a presentation.

AV² was built to bridge the gap between print and digital. We encourage you to tell us what you like and what you want to see in the future.

Sign up to be an AV² Ambassador at www.av2books.com/ambassador.

Due to the dynamic nature of the Internet, some of the URLs and activities provided as part of AV² by Weigl may have changed or ceased to exist. AV² by Weigl accepts no responsibility for any such changes. All media enhanced books are regularly monitored to update addresses and sites in a timely manner. Contact AV² by Weigl at 1-866-649-3445 or av2books@weigl.com with any questions, comments, or feedback.